ONCE UPON A TIME in BIRMINGHAM

WOMEN WHO DARED TO DREAM

OTHER TITLES FROM THE EMMA PRESS

POETRY ANTHOLOGIES

This Is Not Your Final Form: Poems about Birmingham

The Emma Press Anthology of Aunts

The Emma Press Anthology of Love

Some Cannot Be Caught: The Emma Press Book of Beasts

In Transit: Poems of Travel

BOOKS FOR CHILDREN

Queen of Seagulls, a picture book by Rūta Briede

The Book of Clouds, by Juris Kronbergs (illustrated by Anete Melece)

The Noisy Classroom, by Ieva Flamingo (illustrated by Vivianna Maria Staņislavska)

Moon Juice, by Kate Wakeling (illustrated by Elīna Brasliņa)

FICTION PAMPHLETS

Postcard Stories, by Jan Carson (illustrated by Benjamin Phillips)

First fox, by Leanne Radojkovich (illustrated by Rachel J Fenton)

The Secret Box, by Daina Tabūna (illustrated by Mark Andrew Webber)

Me and My Cameras, by Malachi O'Doherty (illustrated by Emma Wright)

POETRY PAMPHLETS

Dragonish, by Emma Simon

Pisanki, by Zosia Kuczyńska

Who Seemed Alive & Altogether Real, by Padraig Regan

Paisley, by Rakhshan Rizwan

THE EMMA PRESS PICKS

The Dragon and The Bomb, by Andrew Wynn Owen (illustrated by Emma Wright)

Meat Songs, by Jack Nicholls (illustrated by Mark Andrew Webber)

Birmingham Jazz Incarnation, by Simon Turner (illustrated by Mark Andrew Webber)

Bezdelki, by Carol Rumens (illustrated by Emma Wright)

once
upon
a time
in
Birmingham
Women
who
dared
to
Dream

THE EMMA PRESS

THE TEAM

Written by Louise Palfreyman

Edited by Philippa Barker

Proofread by Charlotte Geater

Illustrated by Jan Bowman, Yasmin Bryan, Amy Louise Evans,
Saadia Hipkiss, Farah Osseili, Chein Shyan Lee and Michelle Turton

Cover design by Jan Bowman

Text design and typesetting by Emma Wright

Supported by Birmingham City Council

CONTENTS

● ● ● ● ● ●

Birmingham Remembers vii

Aliyah Hasinah 2

PC Andrea Reynolds 4

Asha Devi 6

Barbara Walker 8

Bertha Ryland 10

PC Cath Hannon 12

Catherine Osler 14

Clare Rowland 16

Constance Naden 18

Constance Smedley 20

Denise Lewis 22

Dame Elizabeth Cadbury 24

Dame Ellen Pinsent 26

Hannah Sturge 28

Dr Hilda Nora Lloyd 30

Imandeep Kaur 32

Jessie Eden 34

Joyce Green 36

Joye Beckett 38

Kit de Waal 40

Professor Lea Pearson 42

Lisa Clayton 44

Malala Yousafzai 46

Marion Tait 48

Mary Lee Berners-Lee 50

Professor Pam Kearns 52

Raj Holness 54

Salma Zulfiqar 56

Dr Sara Jabbari 58

Shabana Mahmood 60

Write your own stories 65

Interview someone you admire 68

Go discover! 76

Helplines and support 78

About the writer 81

Acknowledgements 81

About the illustrators 83

Notes from the Spark Young Writers selection team 90

About the Emma Press 93

Other books from the Emma Press 96t

At the start of 2018, the **Birmingham Remembers** campaign was launched to celebrate and commemorate two significant centenaries: the end of the First World War and the success of the women's suffrage campaign, as women over the age of 30 (with certain restrictions) finally got the vote.

One hundred years on from these historic milestones, we wanted to inspire the next generation of achievers, leaders and trailblazers to pursue their dreams. This is how our idea for the book began.

To find 30 inspiring women to profile, we launched a social media drive to crowdsource public nominations, in the hope this would reveal untold tales of ordinary women living extraordinary lives.

We weren't disappointed: the nominations were a mix of historical, contemporary, familiar and unknown women. This made the final selection process very tough, so we brought in a team of young female writers from Writing West Midlands' **Spark Young Writers** groups to help pick the women featured in this book.

Within these pages you will find stories of athletes, campaigners, pioneers, police, engineers, artists and medics – all true and all inspiring.

Once Upon A Time In Birmingham: Women Who Dared To Dream has been created and curated with female-run publisher **The Emma Press**, author **Louise Palfreyman** and **Writing West Midlands**. It was launched as part of the **Birmingham Literature Festival** in October 2018.

COUNCILLOR BRIGID JONES
Deputy Leader of Birmingham City Council,
Bournbrook and Selly Park Ward

COUNCILLOR DEIRDRE ALDEN
Edgbaston Ward

COUNCILLOR MORRIAM JAN
Perry Barr Ward

ALIYAH HASINAH

*A*fter Philando Castile and Alton Sterling were shot by police officers in the USA in 2016, poet and producer Aliyah Hasinah co-organised a demonstration in Birmingham in just 48 hours.

Working with her friend Olivia Brown, Aliyah saw Black Lives Matter (BLM) take to the streets after word spread on social media. More than 1,000 people gathered outside the Bullring, sitting in silence with tape over their mouths and placards held high. The crowd then marched to Steelhouse Lane police station.

'The message of BLM deeply resonates with us,' says Aliyah. 'In Birmingham, literally on our doorstep, young black people have been subjected to police violence.'

Aliyah has always believed everyone has the right to speak their truth. In 2015, she set up Herstory LIVE, a performance night for the forgotten histories of the diaspora. Her work as a curator, poet and arts producer is deeply political and designed to shift power dynamics. She challenged British colonial history with other women of colour, co-curating *The Past is Now* at Birmingham Museum and Art Gallery. The exhibition sought to start alternative conversations to the dominant Western European perspective, re-imagining systems that have historically oppressed people.

Aliyah is particularly tired of the tokenism she sees every October during Black History Month: 'Black history is important all year round, and artists should get work based on their talent, not just ticking boxes for evaluation forms.'

She works to amplify local poets' voices on the national stage as Midlands Producer with Apples and Snakes, an organisation which promotes poetry and performance. She has also explored intersectional dialogue and politics for the schools project *Fearless Futures*.

'THE USE OF ART AS A VESSEL
IS AS VALUABLE AS PEOPLE
WRITING ACADEMICALLY.'
— *ALIYAH HASINAH*

PC ANDREA REYNOLDS

Andrea Reynolds helped change the face of British policing after institutional racism was uncovered during a now-famous murder case. In 1993, black teenager Stephen Lawrence was stabbed to death by a gang in London. Mistakes were made in the investigation, and it took a long time for any convictions to be made.

'Things were at boiling point,' Andrea remembers. 'Stephen's parents were campaigning for their son's death to be properly investigated. At the same time, I was challenging racism within the police force.'

There were very few black officers at the time. Andrea became a regular police officer after failing to gain a place on West Midlands Police's graduate programme, despite having a degree. When she encountered discrimination she challenged it, working with colleagues to establish the West Midlands Black Police Association and later the National Black Police Association.

'It was about sitting together and tackling institutional racism. I was also trying to bridge the gap between the police and my community. I've seen a lot of change in my 24 years of policing. There is at least a legacy from the officers who challenged the force to be more inclusive.'

Andrea has served Sparkbrook and Balsall Heath for eight years and won many awards, including the International Association of Women Police's Officer of the Year. She sees the devastating impact of racial tensions every day.

'The treatment of our grandparents and parents over the Windrush scandal is having an impact on our young black people. We are seeing a rise in knife and gun crime, and an increase in mental health problems.'

Andrea is sad that history is repeating itself and she is doing her best to steer young people away from bad choices: 'I tell kids about the consequences of criminal conduct. I tell them about the impact on their future lives.'

ASHA DEVI

When the World Trade Center in New York City was hit by a terrorist attack on 11th September 2001, Asha Devi volunteered to help in the search and rescue operations.

She was part of a team of structural engineers who, as building experts, worked to make the site safe after two planes were deliberately flown into the skyscrapers, killing and injuring many people. Asha was one of only a few female engineers brought in.

'We all volunteered to help,' she says. 'We provided support day and night. Sometimes we worked with the cave rescue teams and their rescue dogs to search the debris. It was very quiet… I remember no birds sang.'

As a girl growing up in Handsworth, Asha never could have predicted she would end up receiving a certificate of thanks from the Mayor of New York City.

At school, she was the only girl in her Design and Technology class.

'My family encouraged me to become an engineer, especially my father, who worked in the manufacturing industry. As a young man, he came to England with my grandfather in the 1960s. My grandfather served with the army in India, and his travels intrigued me and opened up the world.'

On leaving school, Asha studied Civil Engineering at the University of Birmingham, and now works for the internationally-renowned engineering consultancy Arup. She has designed on and led many iconic projects in Birmingham and across the world. Her favourites include Brindley Place in Birmingham and the HSBC tower in Canary Wharf, London.

Asha wants to see more women choose engineering, and works as an ambassador promoting the subject in schools. 'It does not matter if you are male, female, or where you have come from… if you can engage with people, they will want to work with you.'

'WHAT DID YOU DO FOR
SOMEONE ELSE TODAY?'
— *ASHA DEVI*

BARBARA WALKER

When she was little, Barbara Walker would spend hours looking at illustrations in children's books.

She grew up in Handsworth, in the African-Caribbean community which is so integral to her work. She loved painting and drawing at school and went on to graduate from the University of Central England in 1996 with a first class degree in Art. Since then, she has become one of the UK's most significant artists.

'I looked at my community and how it was represented,' she says. 'There weren't many paintings in the UK at the time representing the black figure. I wanted to present something other than the typical protest photography, or sporting icons. My studies gave me a visual language in terms of how to see, how to gather, and how to express myself.'

Barbara's work often challenges art world conventions and wider power structures at play. She is known for her huge wall drawings. Washed away at the end of each exhibition, they are a statement on how the black community is often erased from society.

Barbara exhibited in the Diaspora Pavilion at the 2017 Venice Biennale, a major international art festival. Her work examined the role of soldiers from the British West India Regiment during the First World War, and how they have been forgotten.

For her ongoing *Show and Tell* series, she produces portraits of young black men as a comment on how the artist judges their subject, and how we judge each other.

'The work examines stereotyping. I am playing with perception. Through history male artists have objectified women. The work tries to subvert and change that, to challenge it conceptually.'

'ARTISTS HAVE AN OBLIGATION
TO INTERPRET THE WORLD
AROUND THEM.'
– *BARBARA WALKER*

BERTHA RYLAND

*I*t was lunchtime on 9th June 1914 when Bertha Ryland entered Birmingham Museum and Art Gallery with a meat cleaver concealed in her coat.

She walked up to a painting of a boy by George Romney – a fashionable portrait artist at the time – and slashed the canvas three times. The police were called and Bertha was arrested.

We don't know why Bertha chose that particular painting, but we do know what her motives were. She carried a note in her coat pocket which was found after her arrest:

> *I attack this work of art deliberately as a protest against the Government's criminal injustice in denying women the vote, and also against the Government's brutal injustice in imprisoning, forcibly feeding, and drugging Suffragist militants, while allowing Ulster militants to go free.*

By 1914, violent acts of protest had become more common in the women's suffrage movement, as campaigners grew increasingly frustrated with Parliament and the treatment of suffragettes in jail. Emmeline Pankhurst, a leading figure in the movement, encouraged women to get arrested and raise awareness of the cause.

While she was in Winson Green Gaol awaiting her trial, Bertha went on hunger strike and was subjected to force-feeding – a brutal practice which involved inserting a long rubber tube down the nose and throat and pouring in food (generally liquids). Bertha dug her heels in at her Birmingham court hearing and would not co-operate, stating: 'I refuse to have anything to do with the trial. I refuse to be tried.'

A statement in *The Suffragette* newspaper revealed afterwards that she had a kidney condition and should not have been subjected to force-feeding. Her health meant the trial was postponed and, as war broke out in August 1914, she was released along with all the other suffragettes and the charges were dropped.

'I ATTACK THIS WORK OF ART
DELIBERATELY AS A PROTEST...'
– BERTHA RYLAND

PC CATH HANNON

*C*ath Hannon spent 32 years fighting some of society's worst criminals.

Despite not being very academic at school, she is now a Doctor of Policing, Security and Community Safety.

It all started when, aged 16, she saw an advert for the West Midlands Police Cadets and her aunt encouraged her to apply. Cath barely scraped through selection, because she was below the height requirement. She cried so much that they measured to the top of her hair instead. She says: 'I still have big hair today.'

The cadets boosted her confidence and she started as a bobby on the beat in Handsworth in 1980, rising to become a Detective Superintendent.

Cath has fought paedophilia, kidnappings, terrorism, murders and organised crime. She is most proud of her multi-agency work to protect children and vulnerable adults. Cath's finest achievement was a nine-month undercover investigation into two paedophiles who were caught and sentenced to life imprisonment.

She also developed better support for victims of crime. 'I treated victims and witnesses as I'd want a member of my own family to be treated by the police. I was also able to ask offenders "Why?" – something all victims want answered.'

She adds: 'Being a woman in a male-dominant career meant I had to work very hard to carve out my own niche and reputation. I broke down barriers for myself and others.'

Cath was given a West Midlands Safeguarding Award for her work protecting children. She retired in 2010 and now works with the Police and Crime Commissioner to reduce crime and deliver policing across the West Midlands. Cath is chair of the Victims Commission, which improves services for victims of crime.

ILLUSTRATION BY
YASMIN BRYAN

BULL RI...
CENTE...

POLICE

G70 FP

'I WANTED TO BE THE
BEST I COULD BE.'
– CATH HANNON

CATHERINE OSLER

*W*hen women were first granted the vote on 6th February 1918, Catherine Osler was quick to point out that this didn't include all women.

It's true that the Representation of the People Act was a landmark victory, but it wasn't a victory for everyone. Only women who were over 30, householders, wives of householders, or who held a university degree could vote. Catherine, as President of the Birmingham Women's Suffrage Society, was determined to give voice to the millions of working women left out of the Act.

She wrote an article called 'At Last!' for the *Women Workers Quarterly* magazine, celebrating the victory but pointing out: 'It leaves still unrepresented classes of women who are among the worthiest, most indispensable workers for their country and for their fellows.'

Catherine, as a suffragist, did her campaigning through the written word rather than defying the law like the more militant suffragettes. But she believed every woman had the right to protest and knew how some women suffered for the cause. Birmingham saw some of the ugliest treatment of women in prison. Winson Green Gaol was one of the first to force-feed suffragettes who were on hunger strike, and the city experienced some of the most violent protests. Catherine noted how many suffragettes had 'endured gross insult, maltreatment, torture, death itself...' in the fight for equality.

The year after women (well, some women) got the vote, many of the leading campaigners were rewarded. Catherine was given an honorary degree by the University of Birmingham in 1919 and the Principal paid tribute:

'Only those who have worked with and under her can justly appreciate the patience, wisdom, courage, and unselfish devotion she has put into the work for the cause… and for the general raising of the standard and welfare of all womanhood.'

ILLUSTRATION BY
AMY LOUISE EVANS

'HENCEFORTH WE MAY GO FORWARD
SHOULDER TO SHOULDER.'
– CATHERINE OSLER

CLARE ROWLAND

*C*lare Rowland helped design a new mental health service for young people in Birmingham, after experiencing her own challenges during childhood and adolescence.

'Academic expectations, combined with the pressure to look and behave in a certain way, made my teenage years incredibly tough,' she says.

When Clare went to university in Manchester, she became increasingly aware of the stigma surrounding mental health issues: 'It's weird, because you'd expect someone with depression to disintegrate, but in my final year I managed to graduate with a first class degree and run a half-marathon. It's amazing what you can achieve whilst silently suffering.'

After graduating, Clare decided that she wanted to do something about how we view mental health. Back in Birmingham, she began contacting various mental health charities for opportunities. She discovered that the Children's Society were looking for young people with experience of mental health issues to develop a new service for the under 25s.

Clare spent several years helping to create what is now known as Pause, designing the space and interviewing staff. She works at their drop-in centre in Digbeth, supporting young people from Birmingham who reach out for help.

'The whole space is welcoming and friendly. You can come in, have a look around, have a hot chocolate. If you want to chat to someone about what's going on, then we're here. We're entirely drop-in based, so you literally just walk in. We know that three out of four mental health issues start in childhood. We want to encourage young people to come and talk to us early on about how they are feeling.'

One young person said: 'If I hadn't come to Pause, I would have contemplated death. When you think about that, it's so huge.'

ILLUSTRATION BY
AMY LOUISE EVANS

'I USED MY OWN CHALLENGES
TO MAKE POSITIVE CHANGES
FOR OTHERS.'
– CLARE ROWLAND

CONSTANCE NADEN

Constance Naden was born in 1858 in Edgbaston, at a time when women were expected to raise a family and engage in gentle, "ladylike" pursuits.

But Constance had other ideas. She went on to become one of the greatest freethinkers of the 19th century. She developed her own philosophy, called Hylo-Idealism, which sought to unify different ways of thinking about the world. Her ideas took hold when she entered into a long correspondence with a retired army surgeon, Robert Lewins. Constance became the first ever female associate at Mason Science College, which later became part of the University of Birmingham. She won prizes for her scientific work and sometimes disguised the fact she was a woman when submitting her writing.

She believed each individual has a unique take on the universe, brought to us via our nervous system – rejecting any notion of a God, or soul. Challenging the religious ideas of the day was pretty revolutionary, especially coming from a woman. But Constance had learned from a young age to be independent in thought and deed. She never knew her mother, who died two weeks after she was born, and was raised by her maternal grandparents.

She travelled extensively, first in Europe and later in the Middle East and India with a friend, Madeline Daniell. On their return, the friends lived together in London, where Constance lit up philosophical circles with her fierce intellect.

Constance was also a great poet, writing about scientific and philosophical subjects. She published her first volume, *Songs and Sonnets of Springtime*, in 1881 and a second volume in 1887.

But it all came to a sudden and tragic end. Constance died after a short illness in 1889, aged only 31. Her memory is honoured each year by the Faculty of Arts at the University of Birmingham when they award the Constance Naden Medal for the best MA thesis.

ILLUSTRATION BY
CHEIN SHYAN LEE

'MAN IS THE MAKER OF HIS OWN
COSMOS, AND ALL HIS
PERCEPTIONS...'
— CONSTANCE NADEN

CONSTANCE SMEDLEY

*C*onstance Smedley is described by the Lyceum Club – which she founded in 1903 – as a 'proud Brummie, an internationalist, a feminist and suffragist.' But it doesn't stop there. She was also a stage designer, illustrator, journalist, novelist, playwright and activist.

Constance grew up in Handsworth and was educated at King Edward VI High School for Girls. She reported on the suffrage campaign, wrote essays on feminism, and had her first illustration published in *The Pall Mall Magazine* when she was just 16.

Her writing dealt with the women's issues of the day and her first novel, *An April Princess*, was described as 'one prolonged flash of brilliancy.'

But women still found it hard to get ahead in the arts, and Constance wanted to establish a place where she and her friends could thrive.

Her father agreed to pay for a building, but only if she signed up 1,000 women as members at a guinea a year. She succeeded and the London Lyceum Club was born! When it took over the former British Imperial Service Club, the sight of women crowding the balconies caused uproar in the male-dominated press. The Lyceum became a stronghold for women's rights and established branches in Amsterdam, Berlin, Paris, and Florence.

In 1909, Constance married artist and poet Maxwell Armfield. Theirs was an unconventional partnership as Maxwell was gay. Husband and wife supported each other in their artistic endeavours, using the international network started by Constance to advance their ideas.

They spent time in America, establishing the Greenleaf Theatre in New York, and were behind community theatre ventures in the Cotswolds.

The Cotswolds Players theatre company survives to this day and Constance achieved fresh fame recently with the performance of a play based on her life.

ILLUSTRATION BY FARAH OSSEILI

'IT IS SUCH A SENSIBLE AND BEAUTIFUL IDEA TO BIND THE WORLD TOGETHER...'
— *CONSTANCE SMEDLEY*

DENISE LEWIS

*D*enise was born in 1972 in West Bromwich and loved sport at school, especially the long jump. From the age of 13 she trained at Birchfield Harriers athletics club in Perry Barr.

She remembers the first time she saw Birmingham's Alexander Stadium: 'I walked through the door and thought, "Wow, this is it. This is where I want to be."'

She made the heptathlon her event: two gruelling days of hurdles, high jump, shot put, 200 metres, long jump, javelin and 800 metres.

When she won gold at the 2000 Sydney Olympics, an interviewer asked her if she was Superwoman. She is certainly made of strong stuff, but it was more likely down to her vision and determination!

Denise was from a deprived part of town and was brought up by her mum. She watched sports on the television every Saturday and it became not only her obsession, but her life. By her teens, she was training three times a week in Birmingham. She won her first gold medal at the age of 21.

After her Olympics triumph in Sydney, Denise was awarded an OBE and went on to be a sports presenter for the BBC. She has since appeared on Strictly Come Dancing, wowing judges with her Rumba and dancing at the Royal Variety Performance. She was inducted into the England Athletics Hall of Fame in 2011 and her old school in Tettenhall, Wolverhampton, even named their one million pound sports centre after her.

Denise remembers the moment she knew she had won gold at the Olympics. She crossed the line at the end of the 800 metres and saw her name in lights.

'I was beside myself, really happy. I had a sense of pride and the sensation of being a big champion. Being on the podium, you see the flag flying... It's sheer joy.'

'BE THE CHANGE YOU
WANT TO SEE...'
– DENISE LEWIS

DAME ELIZABETH CADBURY

*E*lizabeth was born into a large Quaker family in London in 1858.

Her early years were shaped by passionate debate about religious duty and social reform. She lived out this belief as a young woman, engaging in social work in the London docks and slums of Paris. It was fashionable for wealthy young women to go 'slumming', but Elizabeth wanted to bring about lasting change.

Her chance came when she married George Cadbury in 1888. George had moved his chocolate factory out of the slums of Birmingham to Bournville – the new suburb he had created – in order to improve the living conditions of his workers. Bournville became Elizabeth's great project, in between raising eleven children – six of her own and five from George's first marriage.

The couple shared a strong social conscience, rooted in their Quaker values. The whole family became a powerful force for good, transforming Bournville into a model district of Birmingham. Elizabeth set up the Bournville Village Schools in 1906, and established adult schools and sports societies for the factory workers. Bournville Village Trust attracted national attention, influencing many future 'garden cities'.

Elizabeth's whole life was spent in public service. She was a pacifist and women's rights campaigner, particularly concerned with the health and education of women. She served as a city councillor, headed up numerous unions, and worked with Belgian refugees during the Second World War and the International Council of Women after the war, when she was well into her late eighties. Retirement didn't seem to enter her head.

When she died aged 93, she left 150 relatives, including 37 grandchildren and 49 great-grandchildren! She was described by the *News Chronicle* as one of Birmingham's 'grandest and most outstanding women.'

ILLUSTRATION BY
MICHELLE TURTON

'MOST GOOD DONE IN THE WORLD
IS BY INDIVIDUAL EFFORT.'
— *ELIZABETH CADBURY*

DAME ELLEN PINSENT

*F*rom a young age, Ellen Pinsent showed an interest in how women could contribute to society.

In 1885, four years before suffragette leader Emmeline Pankhurst formed the Women's Franchise League, Ellen – then only 19 – gave a speech to a debating society for women, declaring:

'We may be – most of us – only girls, but we have life before us and none of us knows what battles we may have to fight... Probably it will not be long before women are allowed to vote, and at last they will be obliged to take an interest in the government of their country. I only hope they will not wait until suffrage is granted them, but will begin at once.'

Ellen was true to her word, becoming Birmingham's first female councillor in 1911. She was also an aspiring novelist and featured in an issue of *The Woman at Home*, described as 'a slight, artistic-looking woman, young enough to have a long literary career before her.'

In fact, Ellen was to prove far more influential in the field of politics, particularly public health and education.

Ellen married Hume Chancellor Pinsent in 1888 and had a family. She suffered the loss of two sons in the First World War, one in the trenches on the Western Front, and the other testing war planes in 1918. Despite this double tragedy, Ellen continued in her work.

She pioneered new health legislation, assessing children with special educational needs and shaping education provision in Birmingham. She was made a Dame by King George VI in 1937, but her work has been largely forgotten today. Despite this, her contribution to Birmingham education lives on, and the Dame Ellen Pinsent School in Billesley was established in her memory.

'THE PEOPLE I DISLIKE WHEN I FIRST MEET THEM ARE THOSE WHOM, EVENTUALLY, I LIKE BEST.'
— ELLEN PINSENT

HANNAH STURGE

*H*annah Sturge was at the centre of one of the world's first all-female pressure groups.

"The Ladies Society for the Relief of the British Negro Slave" isn't the catchiest name, but it is one of the earliest examples of female activism.

Hannah was born in 1816, at a time when women had very little power. But she was from a Quaker family, and Quakers believed in equality. They were also very active in the anti-slavery movement.

Hannah moved to Birmingham after she married Joseph Sturge, a campaigner and corn merchant. She hosted meetings of The Ladies Society at their home in Wheeleys Road, encouraging boycotts of slave-produced goods, particularly sugar and cotton. More than 830,000 slaves were held across the British Empire in terrible conditions, as slave-owners grew richer and richer.

Hannah and her friends wrote letters and filled handmade silk bags with anti-slavery leaflets, poetry, and illustrated albums. The bags were sold door-to-door to raise funds, and were even sent to royalty. The role these women played in the politics of the day has largely been forgotten, with men receiving the praise for passing laws that eventually abolished slavery.

A visit from American abolitionist Levi Coffin in 1864 illustrates the power of the women's activities. Coffin addressed a large audience at Hannah's home, explaining how 50,000 displaced former slaves were camped along the Mississippi river, dying of hunger and disease. The story was reported in the *Birmingham Daily Gazette*, word spread across the UK, and by the time he returned to America he had raised more than $100,000 for food, clothes and bedding.

Hannah lived to be 90. She hosted The Ladies Society for more than 60 years. It was a blueprint for female activism, spreading to America and paving the way for every movement since.

DR HILDA NORA LLOYD

*H*ilda Lloyd revolutionised the care of women giving birth in Birmingham, enabling home deliveries to be carried out safely.

She was born in 1891 at home in Moseley Road, Balsall Heath, to a grocer and his wife, and was among the first women to study Medicine at the University of Birmingham. In 1930, Hilda married Bertram Arthur Lloyd, a professor of forensic medicine. By 1934 she was a university lecturer herself – in women's health, which she championed her whole life.

Hilda saved countless lives through her mobile midwife teams who went out to the poorest districts of Birmingham. The teams became known as "flying squads" – though they stuck to the roads to get about. The midwives were equipped with portable gas and air machines, surgical tools, blood supplies, and even a tin of biscuits to keep them going on long shifts.

Hilda described how emergencies were dealt with in a report for the Red Cross in 1951: 'The Surgical Officer receives the call and assembles the team. The hot water bottles are filled, the blood is taken from the refrigerator, and the Flying Squad sets out. We reckon to arrive within half an hour, transported by ambulance.'

She was admired for her skill, speed, and energy as a surgeon and later became the first female professor at the University of Birmingham. She was also the first woman to be elected as President of the Royal College of Obstetricians and Gynaecologists in 1949.

Lesley Regan, who is the current President (and only the second woman elected to the position) said: 'Hilda Lloyd was a woman ahead of her time. The "flying squads" she established provided emergency care to mothers and babies who might otherwise have died; she also encouraged women to enter the specialism and, radically at the time, return to work after having children.'

ILLUSTRATION BY SAADIA HIPKISS

'OUR WORK IS RECOGNISED IN EVERY SPHERE OF HUMAN ACTIVITY.'
— HILDA NORA LLOYD

IMANDEEP KAUR

*I*mandeep Kaur is the co-founder of Impact Hub Birmingham, an organisation which seeks to put people at the heart of solving some of the city's most pressing problems.

Immy used to work for a big charity in London, before moving back to Birmingham and becoming one of the curators of TEDxBrum, a series of inspirational talks on issues affecting society today.

From TEDxBrum grew Impact Hub Birmingham, a crowdfunded social enterprise in Digbeth. After initial opposition to their plans, Immy and her friends raised £65,000 to set up a workspace and community hub. More than 750 people pledged their support and the community continues to grow.

Immy recalls how she used to feel about her hometown: 'I was embarrassed to say where I was from, as people didn't see it in the same way as London. But actually, if I'd taken a moment to look, I'd have spent a lot less time travelling around and a lot more time making incredible things happen in Birmingham.'

Working on TEDxBrum and Impact Hub Birmingham changed the way Immy viewed her city: 'I suddenly realised I was surrounded by people who really cared about wanting to make Birmingham a better place. Suddenly it was a really exciting place to be, but it was clear that there were also real problems in the city.'

Immy works with people from the city council and police force, as well as Hollywood stars and Nobel laureates, to tackle child poverty, unemployment, and social inequality.

'I want to make the place we're from better for everyone who lives there. What the world needs more of is uncensored vision – your wildest dreams, the ones that you believe deep down.'

ILLUSTRATION BY
FARAH OSSEILI

IMPACT
HUB

'BELIEVE IN YOUR VISION.'
— IMANDEEP KAUR

JESSIE EDEN

*J*essie Eden went to work every day in a car components factory, along with thousands of other Birmingham women in the 1920s.

One day she noticed a man was timing her, and she soon realised that her speed was being used to set targets for all the other women she worked with. She was the fastest worker in the Lucas Factory.

The men were even timing how long women spent in the toilet, so they could take this off their pay! Jessie didn't think that this was right, so she led her fellow workers out on strike.

She was a significant figure in the 1926 General Strike, when the whole country staged walkouts over work conditions. Jessie told the *Birmingham Post* how she was challenged by the police at a May Day march when 25,000 people took to the streets:

'They were telling me to go home, but the crowd howled, "Hey, leave her alone!" and then some men came and pushed the policemen away.

'They didn't do anything after that. I think they could see that there would have been a riot. I was never frightened of the police or the troops because I had the people with me, you see. I don't know what I'd have felt like on my own.'

It was 1931 when Jessie led 10,000 women out on a week's strike, a single act which made a massive difference in how women fought for their rights at work. She also staged a rent strike in 1939, with 45,000 council tenants campaigning successfully against rent increases.

Jessie lived for her beliefs, and inspired the writers of hit television series Peaky Blinders to include her as a formidable female campaigner.

The real Jessie was still campaigning as a pensioner in 1969, leading a Birmingham march against the Vietnam War.

ILLUSTRATION BY
MICHELLE TURTON

'I WAS NEVER FRIGHTENED... BECAUSE
I HAD THE PEOPLE WITH ME.'
– *JESSIE EDEN*

JOYCE GREEN

*I*n 1976 there were few women directors in business, but that didn't worry Joyce Green. Two directors at the coffin factory where she worked had died in quick succession, and when nobody else put themselves forward Joyce decided to buy up most of the company shares. She remembered: 'I had to come in on Monday and have a little brandy with a bit of hot water to calm me down… and tell everyone that Mr Floyd had died.'

She was told by some of the men at Newman Brothers that they didn't want a woman in charge. She told them: 'Well, that's the way it is.'

Overnight she went from being company secretary to managing director of a coffin fittings firm, selling caskets and shrouds all over the world.

Joyce steered Newman Brothers through hard times. More people were choosing to be cremated, and the demand for coffins was in decline. Eventually, in 1997, it became clear that the company would have to close down.

The firm didn't go quietly. Quite the opposite in fact, as 1997 was also the year Diana, Princess of Wales, died. The royal undertakers, Levertons, chose to use Newman Brothers' finest brass Gothic handles on the coffin.

Joyce remembered seeing them on the telly: 'They were lifting her coffin into the hearse on ITV, and there was a very quick glimpse of the rose of our top-quality handle. It glinted in the sunlight.'

When production ceased, the factory would have been demolished, but Joyce was determined to preserve it for the public rather than see it converted into flats. The building was listed and Birmingham Conservation Trust took over the restoration of the site.

It took 14 years to raise the money to start renovations, and sadly Joyce died before the Coffin Works became what it is today: one of Birmingham's best-loved museums.

ILLUSTRATION BY
JAN BOWMAN

'NEWMANS BECAME MY FAMILY
IN AN ODD SORT OF WAY...'
— JOYCE GREEN

JOYE BECKETT

*W*ith her mischievous sense of humour and passion for acting, Joye Beckett was loved by everyone in her theatre group.

She set up Festival Arts in 1969 with her husband, Jack. It changed the lives of countless Birmingham teenagers who came to weekly sessions in Selly Oak, and on summer camps in Pembrokeshire.

Her daughter Julie says: 'The kids were often away from home for the first time, and some had difficult backgrounds. She'd draw them out of themselves with her humour and willingness to listen. She could talk to anybody!'

Joye made all the costumes for the shows. She was also the cook, the publicity department, prop department and roadie when Festival Arts went away each year. For many of the children, it was the first time they'd seen the sea, or the stars at night. Joye showed them wild flowers on walks, and introduced them to Shakespeare, George Bernard Shaw, and the medieval mystery plays.

One former cast member remembers: 'She was mum to youngsters who had never known a loving home, living and working with them, her bed in a corner of the costume room.'

Music and acting always played a big part in Joye's life. Growing up in Birkenhead in the 1920s and 30s, she would cycle miles to New Brighton beach with her best friend Beatty to see the Pierrot shows. Later, as a Wren (Women's Royal Naval Service) in the Second World War, the women officers staged performances to entertain each other.

Her daughter Jenny adds: 'Having realised she had a great passion, she made sure she shared it. She believed drama helps you develop, and understand people.'

Joye stayed involved in Festival Arts right up until her death in 2017 at the age of 95. When she received an MBE for her services, she said: 'Festival has been my life's work.'

'THE ARTS INFORM EVERY
ASPECT OF YOUR LIFE.'
— *JOYE BECKETT*

KIT DE WAAL

*K*it says the only writers she read at school were 'dead... And white. And posh.' It took a long time before she realised that she, too, could be a writer.

She was born in Birmingham and went to school in Small Heath. After leaving school, she worked in criminal and family law in Handsworth and later served as a magistrate and on adoption panels.

'No one from my background – poor, black and Irish – wrote books. It just wasn't an option,' she says.

Kit began to read novels aged 23, and worked her way through the classics in her twenties. She started to write stories in 2006 and won awards for her short fiction. Then, in 2016, her first novel, *My Name is Leon,* became an international bestseller. The book tells the story of Leon, a mixed-race boy left with a foster mother after his baby brother – who is white – is adopted.

Kit says: 'I had to constantly think about what he would see, what was important to him, what he would notice being small, being a boy, being in grief... feeling disempowered yet never really having had power in the first place.'

Kit has an Irish mother and a Caribbean father, and has many memories of both communities. But she doesn't just write what she knows: Kit tells big-hearted stories about characters she really cares for.

She also advocates for more working-class writers to be published. Only around 10 per cent of people in the industry are from a working-class background. Kit wants that to change. She set up a university scholarship fund so more people could study creative writing.

But it isn't an 'us or them' situation: 'It's a case of us *and* them,' she says. 'Shove all those other books up a bit and make room on the shelf.'

ILLUSTRATION BY
JAN BOWMAN

'WHY WOULD YOU NOT WANT TO
UNDERSTAND OTHER PEOPLE?'
– *KIT DE WAAL*

PROFESSOR LEA PEARSON

*L*ea Pearson was at the forefront of educational psychology throughout her career. She helped children who experienced problems with their behaviour, learning or mental health to get a fair chance at school.

She was born in Cheshire in 1942 and grew up in Derbyshire, reading Philosophy and Psychology at the University of Hull. As a young single mum, she sat some of the first exams in educational psychology and gained a distinction.

Lea went on to become Chief Educational Psychologist for Birmingham – a position more commonly held by men – and President of the British Psychological Society. Lea was determined to help all children have the best possible experience of education, whatever their difficulties. She reshaped education services and brought out the best in people.

One colleague remembers: 'Psychologists were expected to shape a radical future, to deliver change and to take their teams with them. She had definite ideas as to how services needed to evolve and how children should be assessed.'

Under her guidance, Birmingham became a national leader in providing education for the most vulnerable children in society. Lea ran one of the largest teams of educational psychologists in the country, devoting herself to public service as one of the most brilliant minds educational psychology has known. She went on to be a government advisor for school examinations and even introduced a revolutionary Hungarian treatment for cerebral palsy – called Conductive Education – to the UK.

Her work led to great changes in both education and health. Lea argued early on that vulnerable children were at risk of developing mental health problems, an idea which is now at the forefront of discussions today.

Lea died in 1995, aged 53. In her short life, she proved again and again that she was ahead of her time.

ILLUSTRATION BY
MICHELLE TURTON

'THE RENAISSANCE WOMAN.'
– BRITISH PSYCHOLOGICAL SOCIETY

LISA CLAYTON

(LISA LYTTLETON, DOWAGER VISCOUNTESS COBHAM)

Lisa Clayton made a name for herself by becoming the first British woman to sail single-handed and non-stop around the world.

It all started in the early 1990s, when her boss at a holiday firm invited her to join the crew on his yacht one weekend. She remembers: 'I thought it would be boring. He told me to buy wellies, a jacket, and to bring my passport. It turned out to be the beginning of something.'

Lisa, who was 32 at the time, fell in love with sailing. Things got serious when she read about a record attempt by another woman sailor, Naomi James. She says: 'I knew from that moment I had to sail round the world.'

Nobody took Lisa seriously when she began seeking sponsorship. As she explains: 'You don't just appear from nowhere and start sailing a boat.'

But Lisa did exactly that, leaving Britain in September 1994 on board *Spirit of Birmingham*, which she'd bought as a rusting shell. She had financial backing from the University of Birmingham and took the goodwill of her home city with her. Her refusal to give up came in handy during her 285 days at sea: 'I was just working to keep going, and there was nothing to do but survive.'

The boat capsized seven times, at one point knocking her unconscious, but she came home to a heroine's welcome and a world record.

She told the press: 'I think a lot of people, particularly men, thought that because I was an unknown name and because I am a woman, I was not able to face a challenge like this.'

Lisa has gone on to achieve more amazing things, including walking across Spain for charity. She is full of encouragement for others: 'It's about saying to yourself "Anyone can do this, so why not me?" Just get out there and have a go!'

ILLUSTRATION BY
AMY LOUISE EVANS

'MY BOAT WAS CALLED *SPIRIT OF
BIRMINGHAM* BECAUSE THE PEOPLE
THERE BELIEVED IN ME.'
– LISA CLAYTON

MALALA YOUSAFZAI

*M*alala is known the world over as the girl who was nearly killed for her beliefs. She is the youngest person ever to win the Nobel Peace Prize. On 9th October 2012, a gunman from the Taliban extremist group stormed her school bus in Pakistan. 'Who is Malala?' he shouted, before opening fire, shooting her in the head, neck and shoulder. Fighting for her life, 15-year-old Malala was airlifted to the Queen Elizabeth Hospital in Birmingham, where doctors specialise in treating people injured in conflict zones.

Malala was targeted because she campaigned for the right to an education. The Taliban wanted to outlaw education for girls. From the age of 11, Malala had been speaking out and blogging for BBC Urdu. The death threats began when she was 14.

She recovered from the attempt on her life and made Birmingham her home, studying at Edgbaston High School for Girls and gaining a place at Oxford University in 2017 to study PPE (Philosophy, Politics and Economics).

In 2018 she made an emotional return to Pakistan. She spoke on national television about improving the life chances of girls in her home country:

'For the betterment of Pakistan, it is necessary to educate girls and empower women.'

Her charity, Malala Fund, was set up when she was 16. It has given millions of dollars to speed up progress on girls' education around the world.

She was nominated by Archbishop Desmond Tutu for an International Children's Peace Prize, and was awarded the Nobel Peace Prize in 2014, aged just 17. She said in her Nobel Lecture:

'Sometimes people like to ask me why should girls go to school, why is it important for them. But I think the more important question is why shouldn't they, why shouldn't they have this right to go to school?'

ILLUSTRATION BY
SAADIA HIPKISS

'I TELL MY STORY NOT BECAUSE IT IS UNIQUE, BUT BECAUSE IT IS NOT. IT IS THE STORY OF MANY GIRLS.'
— MALALA YOUSAFZAI

MARION TAIT

*M*arion Tait is an internationally famous ballerina, now helping the next generation of dancers at Birmingham Royal Ballet.

Marion has toured worldwide and danced lead roles in classic productions like Coppélia, The Nutcracker, Romeo and Juliet and Giselle – parts coveted by any girl who dreams of becoming a ballerina.

'It was my mother who first signed me up for ballet classes when I was only three,' Marion remembers. 'She thought it would be a lovely thing for a little girl to do, and I took to it straight away.'

Marion chose to focus on ballet because it was a challenge: 'I did well in all my dance exams but there was something special about ballet. I enjoyed the discipline.'

She spent a large part of her career dancing with Sadler's Wells Royal Ballet, which went on to become Birmingham Royal Ballet (or BRB as it is known in the business). 'The company produced some really cutting-edge ballet. I will always thank Kenneth MacMillan for teaching me that acting should not be acting... it should be real.'

Marion has won a string of accolades as a critically-acclaimed dancer: she was given an OBE in 1992; named Dancer of the Year in 1994; made a CBE in 2003 and she has been nominated for two Olivier Awards. She still takes to the stage on occasion but works largely as the Assistant Director for BRB, teaching and supporting their stars as the company's ballet mistress.

'Ballet isn't easy,' she adds, 'and I relate to all the difficulties dancers face. You work late, so you have to keep your energy up and eat properly. It's a tough life, and only a handful will really go to the top, but it's a fantastic career... and of course ballet has never had any issues with equality. A company male has always been on the same salary as a company female.'

ILLUSTRATION BY
AMY LOUISE EVANS

'BALLET DANCERS ARE
ATHLETES... BUT WE HAVE
TO MAKE IT LOOK EASY.'
— *MARION TAIT*

MARY LEE BERNERS-LEE

*M*ary Lee Berners-Lee was a pioneer of the computing age. She was a freelance programmer before the world knew about computers, or freelancing.

Mary Lee worked on early computer programs in the 1940s and 50s, punching code into paper tape that was then fed into massive machines. As a young mum, she established herself as a software consultant, working from home. She paved the way for millions of women to launch businesses that would fit around family life.

And what a family... Mary Lee is the mother of Sir Tim Berners-Lee, who invented the world wide web. She once proudly described herself as 'the grandmother of the web'.

It's easy to see where Tim got his computing genes. Mary Lee loved maths as a child and won a scholarship to the University of Birmingham. During the Second World War she worked on radar development for the top secret Telecommunications Research Establishment in Malvern. After the war she worked in Australia classifying stars, before returning to the UK.

Mary Lee enjoyed plenty of her own landmark achievements before the internet came along. She was on the team behind the Ferranti Mark I – the world's first commercial computer. At Ferranti, she campaigned successfully for female programmers to be paid the same as men, nearly 20 years before the Equal Pay Act came into force.

She once described programming as problem-solving: 'It's very difficult getting a computer programme right. We used to do a dry run to see what would happen but it wouldn't work on the computer. We'd think it was the machine's fault, and sometimes it was...'

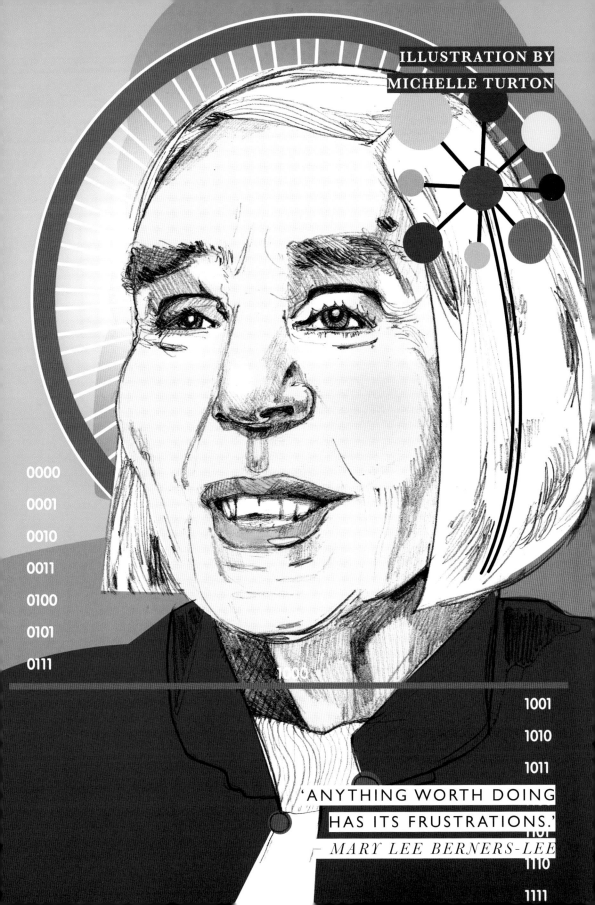

ILLUSTRATION BY
MICHELLE TURTON

0000
0001
0010
0011
0100
0101
0111

1000

1001
1010
1011

'ANYTHING WORTH DOING
HAS ITS FRUSTRATIONS.'
— MARY LEE BERNERS-LEE

1110
1111

PROFESSOR PAM KEARNS

*W*hen parents ask childhood cancer specialist Professor Pam Kearns 'Can you cure my child?' she always wants to be able to reply, 'Yes.'

Pam is one of the UK's top cancer specialists, treating children and teenagers. She decided to become a doctor when she realised she could make a difference to people's lives.

Pam was a shy child at school, but soon found her feet at university in Aberdeen. She did a degree in Physiology, graduating in 1982, and then changed her focus to Medicine, qualifying in 1988. She has never regretted her choice: 'It's the engagement with people I love. What we say and do impacts on every part of a patient's life, and family life too.'

Pam knows medicine can be a tough career choice for a woman:

'You have to learn to become confident in yourself. You aren't achieving "in spite of" being a woman. You are achieving because of who you are.'

Pam now runs the Cancer Research UK Clinical Trials Unit at the University of Birmingham, which was recently awarded nearly £11 million in funding.

'Cancer remains the commonest cause of death in children under 16, so it's crucial we improve treatments,' says Pam. 'But we don't just talk in terms of survival rates. We also need to factor in the side effects, and how having cancer impacts on young lives.'

One of her patients, Paige, was just nine when a huge tumour was found in her stomach. She called it 'Beryl the Bump'. Paige was successfully treated, but remembers when she first got the news: 'I didn't really know what cancer was, but when everyone was getting upset and we had to tell people, I realised how serious it was.'

For many families, Pam is a hero. She has saved many lives and is working hard every single day to save even more.

ILLUSTRATION BY
MICHELLE TURTON

'IT'S IMPORTANT WE FIND CURES FOR
CHILDHOOD CANCERS BECAUSE THESE
CHILDREN ARE OUR FUTURE.'
– DR PAM KEARNS

RAJ HOLNESS

Standing up to domestic abuse can take enormous courage.

Raj Holness didn't just survive – she went on to help other women escape their situations. Raj went through 20 years of domestic violence, attempted murder and two attempted forced marriages, before escaping her family and setting up an organisation to help others.

'I suffered silently for years. I ran away twice and the second time I left, I left in an ambulance. That was the last time I saw my family.'

Raj spent two years in and out of women's refuges and remembers there was very little support for her emotional, physical and mental wellbeing: 'I felt so alone and needed so much help, but couldn't find anyone to turn to.'

Her experiences made her determined to reach out to other women like herself. In July 2013 she set up Breaking The Silence, which enables women to overcome the trauma of domestic violence, forced marriage or sex trafficking. Her organisation is also dedicated to raising awareness in the community and among businesses, helping people to spot the signs.

Their flagship holistic support programme, *Building from Broken Pieces,* works with women to help them overcome trauma. Many women have completely turned their lives around because of Raj and her team.

'Statistically, two women are killed each week by a current or former partner and one in three women experience abuse in their lifetime. Without outside help, these circumstances can be hard to escape.'

But women do break free, as the former Lord Mayor of Birmingham, Honorary Alderman Anne Underwood, observed:

'Breaking the Silence has turned around the lives of so many women, and turned them into what they should be, which is powerful, strong, and confident women.'

'LOVE STARTS WITH YOU...'
— RAJ HOLNESS

SALMA ZULFIQAR

She's highlighted humanitarian issues around the world… and now Salma Zulfiqar is spreading a message of peace, respect and tolerance back in Birmingham, too.

Salma saw how hate crimes against immigrants rose following the Brexit vote. Having grown up in a Pakistani family who also experienced racism, she decided to do something about it. She launched the creative Migration Project in 2017 to help women who had recently arrived in the UK. The project tells the human stories of migration.

Salma explains: 'In the 1960s my father was a victim of racist graffiti. "No Blacks – Go Home" was sprayed on the pavement outside his home in Birmingham. More than 40 years later we are seeing an increase in hate crimes. This begs the question: why aren't we making progress in race relations in Birmingham?'

Raised in Small Heath, Salma was always alive to the issues in her community. She carried this interest in the world around her into adult life, becoming one of the first Asian women to work at ITV television news in the 1990s.

'At the time it was a male-dominated, white middle-class environment so I was very much the outsider,' Salma says. 'But it was exciting and hard work, with good opportunities.'

Salma went on to become one of the first female reporters to travel to Afghanistan under the Taliban rule. She worked with the United Nations, covering the plight of women and children.

'Women in Afghanistan have endured decades of discrimination and violence, with the world watching in silence. Travelling there was life-changing for me.'

Salma has since worked around the world with the United Nations to tell refugee and migrant stories through film-making and art.

ILLUSTRATION BY
CHEIN SHYAN LEE

'LIVE AS YOU DREAM.'
– *SALMA ZULFIQAR*

DR SARA JABBARI

*D*r Sara Jabbari is one of the top mathematicians at the University of Birmingham. She is always surprised at how some people still see maths as nerdy, or a subject for boys. She is working hard to change this.

Sara has risen to the top in a largely male field. She says the best thing about her chosen subject is being able to prove something is either right or wrong: 'I enjoy the completeness of maths.'

Sara's dad is an actuary – he uses numbers every day to assess risk for insurance companies – and her mum is a librarian, so you could say that the family is used to making sense of data.

She went to university in Durham and then studied in France on the Erasmus scheme, which allows students to study abroad.

'Even my approach to learning French was mathematical,' she says.

On her return she embarked on a PhD in Nottingham, and it was there that she first started using maths to fight disease.

'Working with biologists opened my eyes to a whole new field,' she remembers. 'It excites me when I think there are so many new things to learn.'

Sara is now a senior lecturer in Applied Mathematics and a member of the Institute of Microbiology and Infection. Her main goal is helping the world beat bugs like MRSA, which causes devastation in hospitals.

Sara designs computer simulations at the University of Birmingham to work out revolutionary treatments for bacterial infections. She runs thousands of scenarios through a program to help predict disease behaviour.

'Antibiotic resistance is a growing threat that is causing problems worldwide,' she says.

'If we don't do something to tackle it, it will put all sorts of medical procedures at risk.'

ILLUSTRATION BY
AMY LOUISE EVANS

'MATHS IS ABOUT PROBLEM-SOLVING
IT OPENS ALL SORTS OF DOORS...'
– DR SARA JABBARI

SHABANA MAHMOOD

Shabana Mahmood grew up in a Birmingham household where politics played a huge role.

'My Dad was very active in the Labour Party, so I grew up leafleting and door-knocking,' she says.

But it was law that first appealed to a young Shabana: 'My dream was to become a barrister, before I even knew what a barrister was.'

She shone at Small Heath School, went to Oxford University, then launched a successful legal career. 'I got the highest mark in my year in ethics, exploring how to make democracy work and your duty to both the individual and your country. A lot of that flows into politics.'

Shabana realised that she wanted to spend more time in her home city. She became Birmingham's first female Muslim MP, for Ladywood, in 2010. As a local politician she fights cuts to police stations, wants better legal representation for migrants, and helps constituents with housing problems.

'It can be hard sometimes. You want to wave a magic wand and that isn't always possible.'

She has always had an awareness of her status as a member of an under-represented ethnic group and adds: 'When I first came to Parliament it was a culture shock. But if you know why you want to become a politician, then people should not treat you any differently to candidates of any other background.'

The trick, Shabana reckons, is to pretend you are more confident than you really are: 'You have as much right to be there as anyone else. It's important to stand tall, to give a firm handshake, and lots of eye contact.'

Shabana's faith is also important to her. She says of observing Ramadan in Westminster: 'I find the exercise of abstinence empowering.'

ILLUSTRATION BY
CHEIN SHYAN LEE

'IF PARLIAMENT DOESN'T LOOK
LIKE THE PEOPLE THAT IT
REPRESENTS, THEN IT IS NOT AS
RELEVANT AS IT SHOULD BE.'
— *SHABANA MAHMOOD*

Now it's over to you! We've put together some suggestions for writing your own stories and conducting interviews, as well as some lists of helpful websites.

WRITE YOUR OWN STORIES

Think about a woman or girl you know.

She doesn't have to be famous, revolutionary or a pioneer in her field. Pick a woman who inspires you – someone you think is a positive force in the world.

Do some research into her, either online or in the library, and have a go at writing her story. Here are some prompts to get you started:

⇨ Think about some of the **role models** in your life: who do you look to for guidance and inspiration?

⇨ What about the women you admire in the media? Is there anyone **on TV or online** whose approach you really like?

⇨ Or you could work backwards: maybe there are women behind some of **your favourite films, songs, inventions and brands**. Have a dig around and see what you can discover!

⇨ Write the story of a **changemaker** – someone whose actions are paving the way for the women and girls of tomorrow.

⇨ Write the story of an inspirational **creator or maker**: think about artists and writers, designers and directors, innovators and inventors…

⇨ Write the story of a woman who fought against **discrimination and prejudice** – who refused to be silenced.

⇨ Write about a woman who refused to let **gender** dictate what she could and could not do…

You can make some notes on the next page!

INTERVIEW SOMEONE YOU ADMIRE

All the women featured in this book were nominated by the public, and then we narrowed the selection down to the final 30 with the help of a special selection team. Is there anyone you think we missed out, or who you would have liked to see in the book? Whose name would you put forward if there was another call for inspirational women, Birmingham-based or otherwise?

Write the story of a woman who inspires you! She could be someone you know, or someone famous. Choose your person and then get in touch with them to ask if they will give you an interview. You can use our set of questions to kick things off, and then write a story using the answers!

❝ Tell me about your early life... what was school like? ❞

❝ Which subjects did you enjoy? ❞

❝ When did you know what you wanted to do? ❞

❝ How did your family and friends and other people around you support you? ❞

" Tell me about
your early career... "

" How did you
develop the
qualities needed for
your work? "

" Did you encounter
any obstacles along
the way? "

" Are there any
beliefs that you
would say you have
lived by? "

" What has been the
highlight of your life
so far? "

" What have you
learned in life? "

" Do you have a message
for people who are just
starting out in your field? "

NOTES

GO DISCOVER!

Are you interested in learning more about some of the people and places in this book? Here's a list of groups, clubs and organisations who can help you achieve your dreams!

Apples and Snakes . . . . applesandsnakes.org/watch

Arts and Refugees Network . . . . platforma.org.uk

Beatfreeks . . . . beatfreeks.com

Big Bang Fair . . . . thebigbangfair.co.uk

Birchfield Harriers . . . . birchfieldharriers.net

Birmingham Archives and Collections . . . theironroom.wordpress.com

Birmingham Museum and Art Gallery . . . . birminghammuseums.org.uk

British Science Association . . . . britishscienceassociation.org/crest-awards/project-ideas

Coffin Works . . . . coffinworks.org

Children's University . . . . childrensuniversity.co.uk

Duke of Edinburgh's Award . . . . dofe.org

Elmhurst Ballet School . . . . elmhurstdance.co.uk

Feminist Library	feministlibrary.co.uk
Festival Arts Drama Group	somc.org.uk
History Workshop	historyworkshop.org.uk
Impact Hub Birmingham	birmingham.impacthub.net
Malala Fund	malala.org
Maths in Education and Industry	mei.org.uk
Maths Nrich	nrich.maths.org
Midland Sailing Club	midlandsailing.club
Royal Academy of Engineering	raeng.org.uk/education
Spark Young Writers	sparkwriters.org
UN Migration Agency	iom.int
Voices of Science	bl.uk/voices-of-science
Writing West Midlands	writingwestmidlands.org
West Midlands Police Cadets	west-midlands.police.uk/your-options/wmp-cadets

HELPLINES AND SUPPORT

If you have been affected by any of the issues in this book, you can contact one of the organisations below.

B-EAT . . . . beateatingdisorders.org.uk **0808 801 0711**

Breaking the Silence . . . . btsuk.org **0121 285 2277**

Brook . . . . brook.org.uk **0121 237 5700**

Cancer Research UK . . . . cancerresearchuk.org **0808 800 4040**

Childline . . . . childline.org.uk **0800 11 11**

Get Connected . . . . getconnected.org **0808 808 4994**

LGBT+ Helpline . . . . switchboard.lgbt **0300 330 0630**

Macmillan Cancer Support . . . . . macmillan.org.uk **0808 808 0000**

Migrant Help . . . . migranthelpuk.org **0808 8000 630**

Mind . . . . mind.org.uk . . . . **0300 123 3393** . . . . **Text 86463**

Muslim Women's Network . . . . mwnhelpline.co.uk **0800 999 5786**

Domestic Violence	nationaldomesticviolencehelpline.org.uk	
		0808 2000 247
NHS	nhs.uk	111
NSPCC	nspcc.org.uk	0808 800 5000
Papyrus	papyrus-uk.org	0800 068 4141
Pause	forwardthinkingbirmingham.org.uk	0300 300 0099
Rape Crisis	rapecrisis.org.uk	0808 802 9999
Safeline	safeline.org.uk	0808 800 5007
Samaritans	samaritans.org	116 123
The Sexual Healthline	nhs.uk/live-well/sexual-health	0300 123 7123
Talk to Frank	talktofrank.com	0300 123 6600 Text 82111
Teenage Cancer Trust	teenagecancertrust.org	0207 612 0370
Victim Support	victimsupport.org.uk	0300 303 1977

Once Upon a Time in Birmingham is the work of many talented women and girls, all contributing their skills to create this special book.

You can find out more about them in the following pages.

ABOUT THE WRITER

Louise Palfreyman writes fiction and nonfiction and has been published in *Best British Short Stories* (Salt Publishing, 2014), the *Bath Flash Fiction Festival Anthology*, and literary journals in the UK and America. She opened the inaugural London Short Story Festival, and was recently the first writer-in-residence at the University of Wolverhampton.

She mentors writers of short fiction and memoir and works with regional arts projects and universities, delivering workshops, community publications, and readings. Louise writes literary fiction and is currently working on a novel.

WEBSITE: louisepalfreyman.com

ACKNOWLEDGEMENTS

Thanks firstly to everyone who nominated someone they knew or a favourite figure from history. Your nominations led to a journey of discovery for everyone involved.

Thank you to Spark Young Writers and Writing West Midlands for ably assisting in the selection process and sharing their views

Thank you to Philippa and Emma at The Emma Press for steadfast editorial guidance, the illustrators, and to Birmingham City Council for conceiving this project and seeing it through to delivery.

A special thank you to Emma Brady at Birmingham City Council, without whom this book could not have happened.

My research was hugely assisted by Nicola Gauld, Clare Stainthorp, Victoria Osborne, Emalee Beddoes-Davis and Helen Smith who shared collective expertise on Bertha Ryland, Catherine Osler, Constance Smedley, Constance Naden, Barbara Walker, and Dame Elizabeth Cadbury.

Heather Heath and Lesley Regan of the Royal College of Obstetricians and Gynaecologists provided archive material on Dr Hilda Lloyd. Graham Stevenson shared some great insights into Jessie Eden.

The staff at Arup helped me tell Asha Devi's story. Sarah Cresswell, Karen Woodfield and The Children's Society gave background on the Pause service in Digbeth, and Sarah Hayes and Josie Wall at The Coffin Works provided archive material on Joyce Green.

Family and former colleagues of our 30 women were also a great help. Thanks to retired Police Sergeant Andy Lewis for providing a career profile for PC Andrea Reynolds, Professor Simon Keynes and Randal Keynes for sharing the family archive of Dame Ellen Pinsent, and Julie Beckett and Jenny Baines for sharing the diaries and illustrations of their mother Joye Beckett. Alwen Watkins and the colleagues of Prof Lea Pearson provided useful and entertaining anecdotes.

Thanks also to the Library of Birmingham archive service, Heddwen Creaney, Emma Boniwell, Jonathan Davidson, Antonia Beck, Impact Hub and TEDx Youth, Tracy Hulbert, Jo Unwin, Zoe Brookes, Jonna Petterson, Deena Butt, Lucy Dowson, Lara Coffey, Sir Tim Berners-Lee, Anna Kessell, Glen TV, Glenda Dunster, Debbie Ringham and Amanda Daniels.

And thank you to my family, and my extended writing family.

LOUISE PALFREYMAN

Now let's meet all the illustrators...

JAN BOWMAN

Jan Bowman is a trained architect and freelance artist. Originally from Scotland via Canada, she lived and worked in Birmingham for 25 years. She is now based in London.

Jan's book THIS IS BIRMINGHAM, a history of the 18th-century Lunar Society, was published by Waverley Books in 2009. It tells the story of the Industrial Revolution and how Birmingham was built by immigrants. It was on Waterstone's Recommended list for nine months and is often presented as an award in Birmingham schools.

Jan is currently seeking a publisher for her second book, *Arthur*, the graphic memoir of an enterprising scout leader and bicycle mechanic who grew up in Birmingham in the shadow of the Second World War.

WEBSITE: janbow.com

INSTAGRAM: janbowartist

YASMIN BRYAN

Yasmin Bryan has always been interested in the arts, following in the footsteps of her creative family from a young age. She studied the arts throughout school and college, and later graduated with a degree in Visual Communications from Birmingham City University.

Yasmin now lives in Nottingham and works as a freelance designer in print design, card design and commission-based work.

Though her preferred method of practice is digital design, Yasmin also enjoys painting and drawing.

She enjoys creating her own textures in wet media or from photographs, incorporating them into her work.

WEBSITE: yasminnbryan.myportfolio.com
INSTAGRAM: yasminbryanillustrations

AMY LOUISE EVANS

Amy Louise Evans is an illustrator living and working in the West Midlands.

Her style is a mix of hand-drawn and digital artwork, with a focus on people, plants, and the occasional cat. She mainly illustrates for publishing.

In 2013, while she was studying MA Digital and Visual Communication at the University of Wolverhampton, Amy moved into a canal boat right in the centre of Birmingham. She fell in love with everything about Birmingham: its eclectic collection of buildings, its community spirit and the fact that every suburb is heaving with history and character.

WEBSITE: amylouiseevans.com

SAADIA HIPKISS

Saadia Hipkiss is a mixed-media artist based in Birmingham.

Born in Stourbridge, she spent her formative years in Spain before returning to her roots to study at Birmingham City University, where she graduated in Visual Communications – specialising in illustration.

Saadia's style of art is very colourful, using a wide variety of materials including paint, digital art and even papier-mâché.

Saadia has exhibited her artwork far and wide, from Spain's Costa Blanca to Gaudi's Casa Batlló Museum in Barcelona, to London's Brick Lane Gallery and most recently at Newhampton Arts Centre in Wolverhampton.

WEBSITE: behance.net/saadiahipkiss28

CHEIN SHYAN LEE

Chein Shyan Lee is an illustrator based in Malaysia. She is a graduate of Birmingham City University, with a BA (Hons) in Visual Communications, specialising in illustration.

Her interests include children's book illustration, editorial, reportage drawing, branding, printmaking and embroidery. Her work reflects her persistence and attention to detail.

WEBSITE: behance.net/cheinshyan

INSTAGRAM: cheinshyan

FARAH OSSEILI

Farah Osseili moved from Lebanon to Africa to London, but Birmingham is where she now calls home.

Farah graduated with a degree in Visual Communications from Birmingham City University in 2017.

As an artist, she is quite flexible, able to turn her hand to most things, but her passion lies in illustration.

Farah has created a book celebrating women, called *Womanhood*. She draws much of her inspiration from nature and the tranquility it brings her. She wishes to bring that feeling into her work.

WEBSITE: behance.net/FarahOss

INSTAGRAM: far.too.fafi

MICHELLE TURTON

Michelle Turton is a Birmingham-based freelance illustrator, specialising in portrait, travel and lifestyle illustration.

Her work has been exhibited across Europe and has featured in books, on walls, skateboard decks, giant 3D sculptures and walls across the world.

Closer to home, you'll find her work displayed at The Garrick Theatre in Lichfield and exhibited as part of the inaugural Birmingham Design Festival in 2018.

Michelle's 'Peony Passion' sun bear sculpture, which she painted for The Big Sleuth art trail in 2017, raised £8,000 for Birmingham Children's Hospital.

WEBSITE: michelleturton.com

INSTAGRAM: michelleturton

Finally, let's hear from our selection team!

Spark Young Writers Groups are run by Writing West Midlands across the region and are for children and young people interested in any kind of creative writing. We invited some girls from these groups to help us decide on the final selection of women for this book.

How many famous Brummie women can you name? Exactly. This is such a fascinating city yet – much like the female gender – it's often shoved into second place. Second city; second sex. With this book, we hope to change that.

Greater recognition will come with social change. The two go hand-in-hand. In order to achieve greater awareness of the work of women, we must strive for a world in which woman and man are defined by strength of character and action. The women we have chosen have fought, often against discrimination or prejudice, to achieve things that have earned them a place between these pages.

EVE CONNOR, AGED 14

This book raises awareness of women's rights by celebrating the underrated champions of our society – women who have made a strong impact on so many lives in our city. This book will uphold their cause and highlight their contributions, which might in turn inspire many young women to pursue similar efforts.

IONA MANDAL, AGED 12

All of the women in this book are true pioneers and excellent role models. We wanted to help promote the achievements of women and how much of an influence they are on our daily lives. There should be more books and award ceremonies to celebrate the success of women all over the world.

MILJA STEVENSON, AGED 13

Many of these women are unsung heroes. I was astounded by how few I had heard of before. It seems that few care to acknowledge the achievements of women; to remedy this, we need to celebrate women's attainments, past and present. Change starts small. Simply taking a moment to congratulate the capable women around you can have a positive effect.

MARYAM ALTAMANE, AGED 15

All the women in this book are determined, conscientious and fearless.

JASMINE SANDHAR, AGED 17

I think that it's crucial the history of Birmingham, our home, is told. I think it's good that people are going to be able to learn about a variety of inspirational and important women, who despite their differences, all have links to the same city.

SCARLETT CLAYTON-BULL, AGED 15

Women like Clare Rowland, Andrea Reynolds, Mary Lee Berners-Lee, Hilda Lloyd and Hannah Sturge all showed acts of courage as they went against the stereotypical beliefs of their times.

ALICE TYLER, AGED 13

Determination and passion are the two most important characteristics these women share. Passion is necessary to want to create change, and determination is what leads people to persevere when they face difficulty, discrimination or prejudice.

CAITLIN SMITH-MURPHY, AGED 15

OUR SPARK YOUNG WRITERS SELECTION TEAM

Eve Connor (14), Iona Mandal (12), Milja Stevenson (13), Maryam Altamane (15), Jasmine Sandhar (17), Scarlett Clayton-Bull (15), Alice Tyler (13), Caitlin Smith-Murphy (15), Gabrielle Griffiths (14), Zahra Hafedh (13), Aoife Kerr (13), Maisy Mansell-Warren (13), Hamnah Manzoor (15), Ikran Osman (15), Jess Sandhar (14)

ABOUT THE EMMA PRESS

The Emma Press is an independent publishing house based in the Jewellery Quarter, Birmingham, dedicated to producing beautiful, thought-provoking books. It publishes themed anthologies, single-author pamphlets, translations and books for children, usually illustrated.

The Emma Press was founded in 2012 in Winnersh by Emma Wright, with the support of the Prince's Trust. The first Emma Press book, published in 2013, was *The Flower and the Plough*, a collection of love poems by Rachel Piercey. Since then the Emma Press has published over 50 titles.

The Emma Press won the Michael Marks Award for Poetry Pamphlet Publishers in 2016, having been shortlisted in 2014 and 2015. Emma Press books have also won the Poetry Book Society Pamphlet Choice Award, the Saboteur Award for Best Collaborative Work, and the CLPE award for children's poetry books, CLiPPA.

The Emma Press is keen on making poetry welcoming and accessible. In 2015 they received a grant from Arts Council England to travel around the country with Myths and Monsters, a tour of poetry readings and workshops aimed at children aged 8+. They run lots of events and workshops, as well as regular calls for submissions to their anthologies and poetry pamphlet series.

theemmapress.com

emmavalleypress.blogspot.co.uk

Here some highlights from the

Emma Press story so far...

New poetry press aims to connect with readers

21.01.13 | Charlotte Williams

The Flower and the Plough

f Share 158   **in Share** 0   **g+1** 0   **Tweet** 133

A new poetry press aiming to focus on the consumer relationship has been launched by Emma Wright, who previously worked at Orion. Its first book will be released at the end of the month.

January 2013:
The *Bookseller*
announces the
arrival of a new
publishing house!

June-August 2013,
Lower Marsh Market:
Emma runs a weekly
poetry book stall over
the summer, selling the
first Emma Press book
as well as books by
fellow indie publishers.

August 2015:
The Emma Press is
awarded funding from
Arts Council England,
to run the Myths and
Monsters children's
poetry tour.

Monstrous good fun for youngsters at workshop

...with children at Slough Library

CHILDREN were treated to a poetry tour of myths and monsters, alongside a visit from an award winning poet.

Joseph Coelho, winner of the 2015 CLPE Poetry Award visited the Slough Library as part of workshops which include poetry readings, interactive storytelling and poetry writing, on Tuesday.

Brought to Slough by Emma Press publishing company, the theme of "myths and monsters" came from the company's first children's book, Falling Out of the Sky: Poems about Myths and Monsters, edited by Rachel Piercey (Newdigate Prize 2008) and Emma Wright.

December 2016,
The British Library:
Emma gives a speech
just before winning
the Michael Marks
Award for Best Poetry
Pamphlet Publisher.

July 2017, National
Theatre: *Moon Juice*, a
children's poetry book
by Kate Wakeling,
with illustrations by
Elīna Brasliņa, wins
the CLiPPA!

L-R: YEN-YEN LU, RACHEL
PIERCEY, EMMA WRIGHT, KATE
WAKELING, ELĪNA BRASLIŅA

July 2018, Frilly
Industries: The Emma
Press publishes its first
children's picture book,
Queen of Seagulls by Rūta
Briede. Rūta visits the
UK from Latvia to
do some readings in
schools, and also runs
a workshop for the
Birmingham Originals
Etsy team.

If you enjoyed
this book, here
are some more
Emma Press titles
you might like!

THE EMMA PRESS ANTHOLO...

BEST FRIENDS FOREVER POEMS ABOUT FEMALE FRIENDSHIP

THE SECRET BOX   DAINA TABŪNA

...S ☆ POEMS ABOUT SPACE AND...

THE NOISY CLASSROOM ❄ IEVA FLAMINGO

POSTCARD STORIES   JAN CARSO...

THE EMMA PRESS ANTHOLOGY OF MOTHERHOO...

FIRST FOX

THE EMMA PRESS ANTHOLOGY OF THE SEA

THE EMMA PRESS ANTHOLOGY OF AGE

HOMESICKNESS AND EXILE POEM...

THE EMMA PRESS ANTHOLOGY

THE EMMA PRESS ANTHOLOGY OF FATHERHOOD

JAMIE McGARRY   THE DI...

FALLING OUT OF THE SKY ☆ POEMS ABOUT...

MOON JUICE ☆ POEM...

URBAN MYTHS AND LEGENDS ...

THE EMMA PRESS ANTHOLOGY OF DANCE

The Secret Box

Short stories by Daina Tabūna
Translated by Jayde Will
With illustrations by Mark Andrew Webber

On the cusp of womanhood, Daina Tabūna's heroines are constantly confronted with the unexpected. Adult life seems just around the corner, but so are the kinds of surprise encounter which might change everything.

Two siblings realise they're too old to be playing with paper dolls. A girl develops a fixation with Jesus. And a disaffected young woman stumbles into an awkward relationship with an office worker. The narrators of these three stories each try, in their own way, to make sense of how to behave in a world that doesn't give any clear answers.

ISBN 9781910139905

RRP £6.50

Paisley

Poems by Rakhshan Rizwan
With an introduction by Leila Aboulela

'I feel as if I've been waiting for these poems.' Moniza Alvi

Rakhshan Rizwan's debut collection simmers with a poised, driving anger. Drawing on the rich visual and material culture of her home region, Rizwan unpacks and offers critical comment on the vexed issues of class, linguistic and cultural identity – particularly for women – in the context of Pakistan and South Asia.

She writes about the hypocrisy of the men who claim to worship women, the nuances of using Urdu or Hindi, and the many contradictions of the city of her birth, Lahore.

ISBN 9781910139783
RRP £6.50

Best Friends Forever

Edited by Amy Key

★　　★　　★

'A moving, funny, wise and important showcase of intense sisterhood.' Emma Jane Unsworth

This anthology reflects the scale of intensity within female friendships and captures the defining characteristics of this frequently-overlooked relationship: the intimate and the casual, the life sustaining and the life changing, as well as the tensions and the joys.

This book celebrates the transformative power of friendship among women, considering the moments where friendships are 'made', the relationship between friendship and romantic love and friendship and rebellion, the role of culture – fashion, cinema, music, art – in forming friendships, and feelings towards friendships lost or regained.

ISBN 9781910139073

RRP £10.00

First fox

Short stories by Leanne Radojkovich
With illustrations by Rachel J Fenton

'Simple, but wonderfully so, telling the reader all they need to know. Radojkovich's writing knows where embellishment is needed, and recognises when sparse language is effective.' Sabotage Reviews

'startlingly honest, warm and at times darkly humorous'
Literature Works

The stories in *First fox* offer an everyday world tinged with the dreamlike qualities of fairy tales. Radojkovich explores the complex dynamics of families with a blend of dry wit and startling imagery. Disappointments and consolations meet with fantastical moments, winding their way into the realm of possibility.

ISBN 9781910139707
RRP £6.50

Postcard Stories

Short stories by Jan Carson
With illustrations by Benjamin Phillips

★   ★   ★

*'These small snapshots of the ordinary become extraordinary when
painted with her words.'* Jackie Law

'Carson's mini-stories show a wonderful flight of imagination' Nudge Book

Each day of 2015 Jan Carson wrote a short story on the back of a
postcard and mailed it to a friend. Each of these tiny stories was inspired
by an event, an overheard conversation, a piece of art or just a fleeting
glance of something worth thinking about further.

In this collection of highlights, Carson presents a panoramic view of
contemporary Belfast – its streets, coffee shops, museums and airports –
through a series of small but perfectly formed snapshots of her home.

ISBN 9781910139684

RRP £6.50

Malkin

Poems by Camille Ralphs
With illustrations by Emma Wright

★ ★ ★

*'An engagingly inventive pamphlet bringing the Pendle story to life
through innovative language, which dazzles and enthrals.'*
Judges for the 2016 Michael Marks Awards

Malkin is a vivid evocation of the trials of the Pendle Witches in 1612. The sequence of poems is delivered in the form of epitaphic monologues, with the accused men and women eerily addressing the reader with their confessions and pleas.

Strikingly, Camille Ralphs has employed unorthodox spelling throughout the monologues, bringing out new meanings in familiar words and encouraging the reader to immerse themselves in the world of the poems.

ISBN 9781910139301

RRP £5.00

The Emma Press Anthology of Love

Edited by Rachel Piercey and Emma Wright
With illustrations by Emma Wright

★　　★　　★

In *The Emma Press Anthology of Love*, that familiar four-letter word takes on a world of meanings. Love is transcendent and love is everyday, found equally in steamy texts and shopping lists, and the only reliable thing about it is that it's never where you expected to find it.

Love is transcendent and love is everyday, found equally in a remembered tune, on the seashore or in a cup of tea. Often awkward, never perfect, romantic relationships have been a key subject for poets for centuries. In *The Emma Press Anthology of Love*, fifty-six poets speak to what love means to them right here, right now.

ISBN 9781910139561

RRP £10.00

The Flower and the Plough

Poems by Rachel Piercey

With illustrations by Emma Wright

'wry and sparky and filled with wonderful turns and jumps'
Literature Works

*'Piercey's oscillations between lover's ecstasy and love poet's objectivity
are so deft that her analytical lens becomes as much a fascination as
the amorous perspective which it focuses.'* Oxonian Review

A charming collection of love poems by Rachel Piercey, executed with
her characteristic emotional and linguistic clarity. Romantic but never
sentimental, Piercey builds up a nuanced study of passion and heartbreak
over these twelve poems, capturing everything from the extravagant
surrender of early love to the raw ache and misery that can follow.

ISBN 9780957459601

RRP £5.00